THE
SECRET
THREE

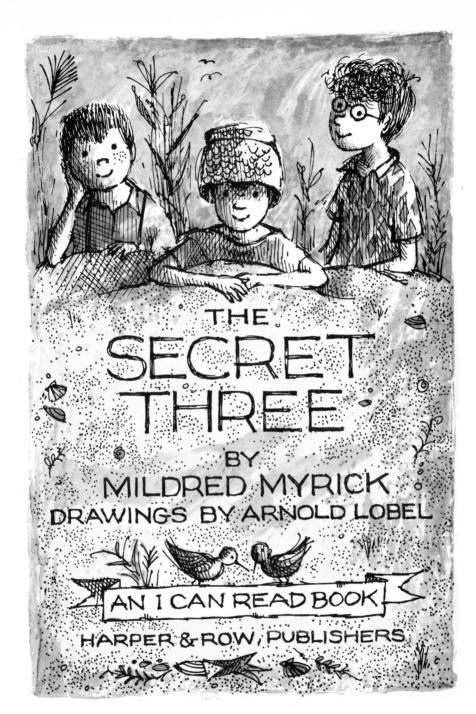

THE SECRET THREE

BY
MILDRED MYRICK
DRAWINGS BY ARNOLD LOBEL

AN I CAN READ BOOK

HARPER & ROW, PUBLISHERS

To J.H.M.,

who has sent many messages

Mark came to stay with Billy
at the beach.
"Let's go for a swim,"
said Mark.
"We have to wait an hour
after we eat," said Billy.
"Let's take a walk on the beach.
The tide was high this morning.
We may find something good
on the sand."

They walked along the beach.

They saw shells.

They saw a starfish.

Billy saw a green bottle

in the seaweed on the beach.

Mark said, "It is nothing

but an old bottle.

Bottles are not much fun."

Billy picked up the bottle.

"Look, Mark!" he said.

"There is writing

on a piece of paper

inside the bottle."

Billy took the paper

out of the bottle.

"I think it is a message,

but I cannot read it," Billy said.

Mark took the piece of paper.

He could not read the writing.

This is what they saw:

I live on the island.
It would be fun to
have a club with
some boys who
can read this
writing.
Tom

The boys took the paper

to Billy's house.

They held the paper upside down.

They held it right side up.

They could not read the writing.

Billy put the paper on a table.

Mark picked up the paper.

"Maybe there is something

on the other side," said Mark.

"No, there is nothing."

"Look in the mirror!" cried Billy.

"Now we can read it!"

This is what they read:

"Let's have a club!

Clubs are fun!" Billy said.

"Yes! We can send secret messages

to each other!" said Mark.

"We could have a name

for our club!" said Billy.

"Secret is a good word," said Mark.

"And there are three of us."

"THE SECRET THREE!" cried Billy.

"That's a good name!" Mark said.

"I hope Tom likes it!"

"When is the next tide?" asked Mark.

"I know," said Billy.

"The newspaper has a chart.

Each day the tide is later.

The tide was high on our beach

at five o'clock this morning.

It will be high again tonight

about half-past five."

The boys worked on a secret message.

They wrote the alphabet.

They put one letter under the other.

Then they gave each letter a number:

a	1	j	10	s	19
b	2	k	11	t	20
c	3	l	12	u	21
d	4	m	13	v	22
e	5	n	14	w	23
f	6	o	15	x	24
g	7	p	16	y	25
h	8	q	17	z	26
i	9	r	18		

This is the message they sent:

Two 2-15-25-19 found your message. We know your name is 20-15-13. Can you tell us our names? Do you think THE SECRET THREE is a 7-15-15-4 name for a club?

13-1-18-11 and 2-9-12-12-25

The boys put the message

in the bottle.

They took the bottle to the beach.

They were just in time.

The tide was starting to go out.

When they could not see the bottle,

Billy and Mark went home.

They looked in the newspaper.

The next high tide was

about six o'clock the next morning.

Billy and Mark were at the beach
at six o'clock.

They did not find the bottle.

"We can look again

after the next high tide," said Mark.

"Maybe Tom could not find

the bottle last night.

Maybe he is finding it right now!"

After supper Billy and Mark

went back to the beach.

They walked a long time,

but they did not find the bottle.

They met a fisherman

working on his boat.

It was named "Kingfisher."

"Are you looking for something?"

asked the fisherman.

"We are looking for a green bottle,"

said Billy.

"I hope you find it," said the fisherman.

Mark and Billy walked on,

but they did not find the bottle.

Billy stopped to pick up a shell.

Mark ran toward something on the beach.

It was the green bottle.

"Hurry, Billy!" cried Mark.

"Here is our bottle,

and there is a paper inside it!"

"You are right!" Billy said.

"It is our bottle,

and there is a message inside!

I can see the writing!"

They opened the bottle.

They took out the paper.

This is what they found:

Your names are Mark and Billy. I had a hard time with your message. THE SECRET THREE can meet on Tuesday. Please come with the fisherman.

Tom

Billy took a mirror from his pocket.

The message said:

Your names are Mark
and Billy. I had a
hard time with your
message. THE SECRET
THREE can meet on
Tuesday. Please come
with the fisherman.

Tom

"I want to go to the island

and see Tom," said Billy.

"I want to go, too," said Mark.

"We can ask the fisherman now."

They told the fisherman about the club.

They showed him the message.

"May we go with you to the island?"

Billy asked the fisherman.

"Yes, if you ask your father,"

said the fisherman.

"When we get to the island,

how will we know which boy is Tom?"

Mark asked.

"We could have a secret sign

and a secret handshake.

When a boy gives the secret sign

and the secret handshake,

we will know he is Tom," said Billy.

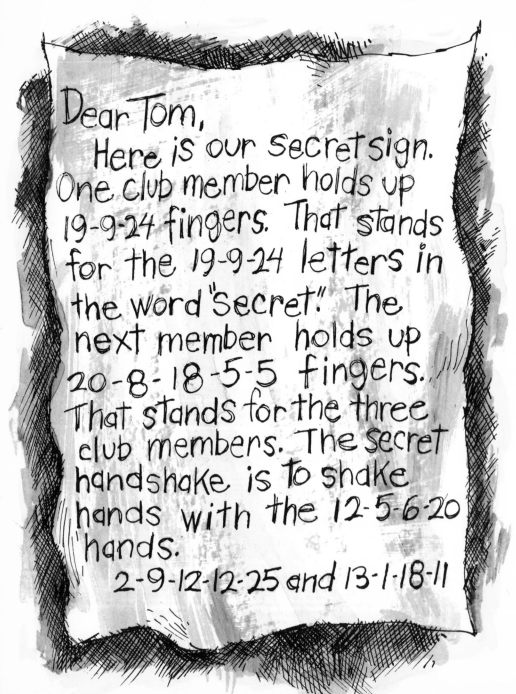

Dear Tom,
   Here is our secret sign.
One club member holds up
19-9-24 fingers. That stands
for the 19-9-24 letters in
the word "secret." The
next member holds up
20-8-18-5-5 fingers.
That stands for the three
club members. The secret
handshake is to shake
hands with the 12-5-6-20
hands.
      2-9-12-12-25 and 13-1-18-11

They put the message in the bottle.

The tide took it out.

On Tuesday they met the fisherman

at the beach.

They liked the ride in the boat.

"We could have an explorers' club
and explore the island."

"Would your father let us explore

the lighthouse?" asked Mark.

"We can do that today," said Tom.

Tom's father showed them the lighthouse.

He showed them the light

that shines for ships at sea.

He showed them the foghorn.

"A lighthouse is fun," Mark said.

"Thank you for showing it to us."

The boys walked over the island.

They found shells.

They saw sea gulls.

They saw sand dunes.

"These dunes would be a good place

to camp all night," said Tom.

"Could we do that?" asked Mark.

"Let's all find out if we can

bring a picnic supper next Tuesday

and camp out," Tom said.

"We can cook our food

the next morning," said Billy.

"I wish next Tuesday

would come now," said Mark.

"I wish every day would be Tuesday,"

said Tom.

"I think we should have

a secret password," said Billy.

The boys thought about one.

They thought about "island."

They thought about "explorer."

"What about spelling

our names backward?" Billy asked.

They tried Krammotyllib.

They tried Yllibmotkram.

They tried Motyllibkram.

"Perhaps we could use just parts

of our names," said Tom.

The boys made up words

with parts of their names.

They made up Bitoma—Tobima—

Ommaly—Kromly—Matobi—

"Matobi!" said all three boys at once.

"Matobi is good.

It sounds like an Indian word,"

said Tom.

Soon it was time for Mark and Billy

to go home.

The boys shook the secret handshake.

They made the secret sign.

"Matobi," said Tom.

"Matobi," Mark and Billy answered.

Tom was waiting for Billy and Mark

the next Tuesday.

They walked down the beach.

"Here's a good place for our tent,"

said Mark.

After the tent was up,

Tom began digging around it.

"Why are you digging?" asked Mark.

"So the water will not come

under the tent if it rains," said Tom.

After supper the boys

took a walk on the beach.

They saw a sea turtle.

"Sea turtles lay their eggs

in the sand at night," said Billy.

"The warm sand hatches the eggs."

"I see the full moon coming up,"
said Mark.

"Then we will have
a very high tide tonight,"
said Tom.

Going to bed in the tent was different
from going to bed in a house.
"Everybody in," said Tom
as he closed the tent.
"I am a giant cocoon," said Mark
when he was inside his sleeping bag.
"We are all giant cocoons,"
Billy said, "and tomorrow morning
we will be giant moths."
"Matobi," said all three boys.
Then they went to sleep.

Mark woke first next morning.

He saw the sun coming up.

He was happy.

He wrote a secret message

in the sand.

This is the message Mark wrote:

Clubs 1·18·5 fun
Friends 1·18·5 fun
I am glad I belong
To THE SECRET THREE.
Matobi

13-1-18-11

When Billy came out of the tent,

he read the message and added

2-9-12-12-25

When Tom came out of the tent,

he read the message and added

20-15-13

"Clubs are fun," said Tom,

"and THE SECRET THREE is

the most fun of all!"

"Matobi!" answered Billy and Mark.